NATIONAL GEOGRAPHIC KiDS

YOGA Animals

Paige Towler ❀ with a foreword by Tara Stiles

A **wild** introduction to **kid-friendly** poses

NATIONAL GEOGRAPHIC
WASHINGTON, D.C.

Foreword

Get ready to stretch, move, and breathe deeply—just like animals do!

Think about all the different ways your favorite animals move: A giraffe stretches her neck high to reach a meal of leaves. A gorilla pounds his chest to communicate with other gorillas. Kittens curl and jump to play. Every day, from the tiniest ant to the largest elephant, animals bend and stretch to find food, protect their families, rest, and even play! All this movement keeps them healthy, strong, and ready for any adventure that might come along.

And just like it is for animals, stretching is good for you, too. When you practice yoga you get to take time just for you, slow down and check in with how you feel, and be present in each and every moment. It's also fun! Yoga lets you stand on one leg like a flamingo, roar like a lion, and hop like a bunny. By copying your favorite animals, you too will be ready for every adventure!

If you are new to yoga, don't worry: Animals are great teachers when it comes to moving naturally. Spend some time watching these fantastic creatures and see how they inspire you to move—there is no right or wrong way! The secret to yoga is remembering that it's right inside you, waiting to be discovered. You can do this. If you can't touch your toes with your legs straight, bend your knees. If you tumble over, sway like the breeze back up. Yoga is not about being bendier or stronger than you are. Yoga is about moving in a way that is fun, natural, and good for your body and mind. Don't worry if you don't follow the instructions in this book exactly—it is more important to have fun and feel comfortable than to get the poses "right." The instructions are there to guide you, so go with the flow and do what feels right!

I love practicing yoga with my daughter, Daisy. We take inspiration from our favorite animals and enjoy all the different ways we can move like them. We take long, deep breaths together. We play, crawl, stretch, and bend, and have tons of fun! Practicing yoga is a great way to discover the awesomeness that is right inside every one of us. It's time to practice being like our animal friends. Enjoy, and remember to breathe deeply!

Big hugs and deep breaths,
Tara Stiles

Tara Stiles and daughter Daisy

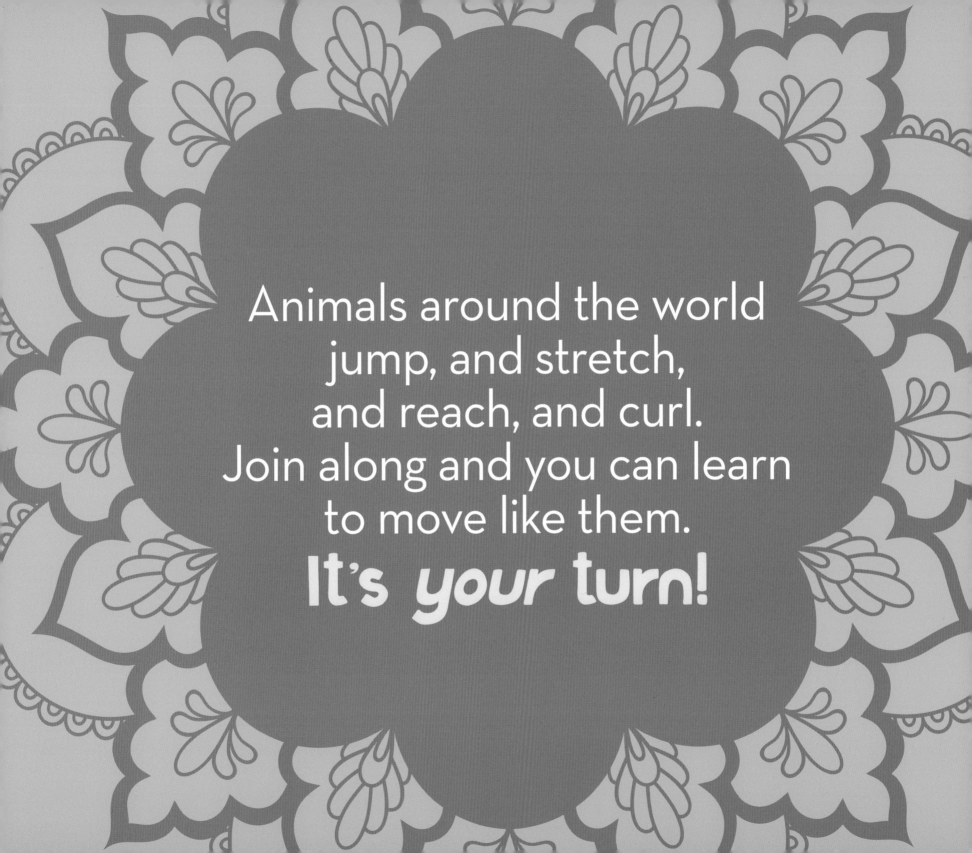

Animals around the world
jump, and stretch,
and reach, and curl.
Join along and you can learn
to move like them.
It's *your* turn!

Young giraffes **reach** to the trees, **stretching tall** for tasty leaves.

REACH
like a giraffe!

Take a big deep breath in and stretch your arms up over your head. You can also bring the palms of your hands together. Keep your shoulders relaxed and feel the top of your head reach toward the sky.

Peaceful pink flamingos **stand,**
balancing in shifting sand.

BALANCE
like a flamingo!

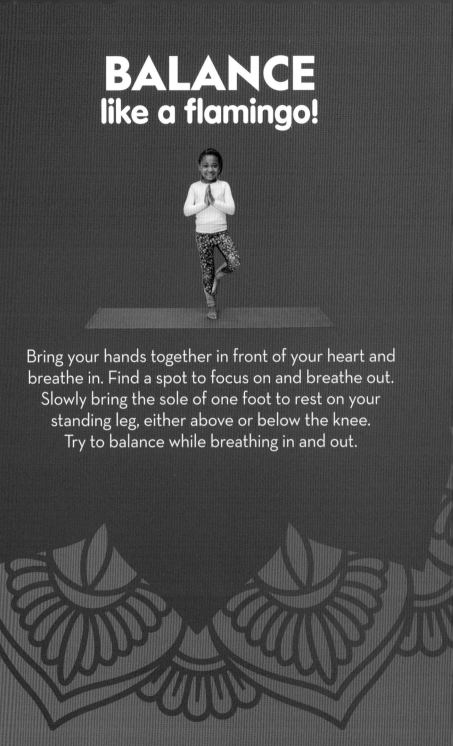

Bring your hands together in front of your heart and breathe in. Find a spot to focus on and breathe out. Slowly bring the sole of one foot to rest on your standing leg, either above or below the knee. Try to balance while breathing in and out.

Loud gorillas **pound** their chests,

bend, and **hang** their arms to **rest.**

BEND
like a gorilla!

Stand with your feet facing forward and slightly apart and take a big deep breath in. Pound your chest and let out a yell! Breathe in again, and when you're ready, breathe out and gently bend forward from your hips, keeping your knees slightly bent. Let your arms and head hang toward the floor. Rest here as you breathe in and out.

Sleepy, cozy cats **relax**,
arch their spines,
and **curl** their backs.

CURL
like a cat!

Come down onto your hands and knees, bringing your hands under your shoulders and your knees under your hips. Take a deep breath in. Breathe out and gently relax the top of your head toward the floor and round your spine upward. Breathe in and arch your spine, dropping your belly toward the floor and raising your head and tailbone up. Do this as many times as you want, breathing in and out.

Playful puppies **run** and **fetch**, **tumble**, **tussle**, **stop**, and **stretch**.

STRETCH
like a puppy!

Start on your hands and knees. Place your palms flat on the floor, shoulder-width apart. Take a big breath in. Breathe out and press down through your feet and gently reach your "tail" up to the ceiling, forming an upside-down V. Relax your head and neck, and breathe in and out at your own pace.

Lions **shake** their manes before **lifting** golden heads to **roar**.

ROAR
like a lion!

Kneel on the floor and sit back with your hips on your heels. Bring your hands to the floor in front of you (or to your knees), and show your "claws" by spreading your fingers wide. Breathe in through your nose. Then open your mouth wide, stick out your tongue, and ROAR by breathing out loudly through your mouth!

Bunnies **bounce** on velvet toes, then **tuck** fluffy tail to nose.

TUCK
like a bunny!

Do some bunny bounces! When you're ready, kneel on the ground and sit back on your heels, tucking your "tail" toward the ground. Lace your fingers behind your back. Take a big breath in. Gently lean forward and relax your body on top of your legs. Tuck your head to rest on the ground in front of you. Gently lift your "bunny ears" by raising your arms behind you toward the sky. Breathe in and out.

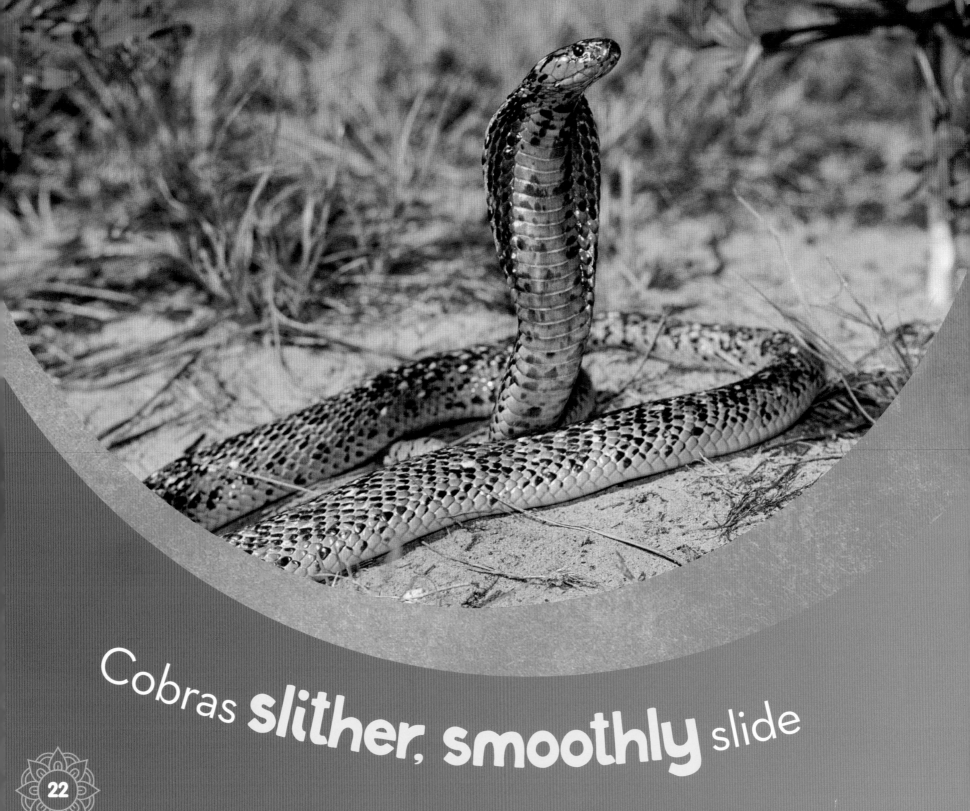

Cobras **slither, smoothly** slide

into nests where they can **hide.**

SLIDE
like a cobra!

Slide onto your tummy with your legs straight out behind you. Place your palms flat on the ground next to your shoulders. Take a big breath in and gently lift your head, chest, and shoulders off the ground. Exhale and lie back down. Repeat as many times as you like.

Crocodiles slowly **creep**

SLEEP
like a crocodile!

Lying on your belly, cross your arms in front of your head. Rest your forehead on your hands or arms, and let your whole body relax. Breathe deeply for six to ten breaths.

on soft and sun-warmed banks to **sleep.**

Creatures all across the land
bounce, and sleep, and slide, and stand.
They reach and leap, just like you:
**Critters stretch.
And you can, too!**

Animal Yoga Guide

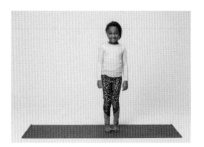

Giraffe (also called upward salute):
Urdhva Hastasana

This pose helps you practice standing up straight and tall! Begin standing with your feet together and your arms by your sides. Take a big deep breath in and reach your arms up over your head, keeping your palms facing each other and your arms parallel to each other. You can also bring the palms of your hands together. Keep your shoulders relaxed and your neck long.

Southern Giraffe

Giraffes are famous for their large brown spots and long necks. They live in grassy plains called savannas in central, eastern, and southern Africa. Their long necks help them stretch high into treetops to reach leaves, seeds, and fruits.

Flamingo (also called tree pose):
Vrksasana

Stand straight and tall, with your shoulders relaxed and your arms by your side. Bring your hands together in front of your heart and breathe in. Find a spot to focus on to help you balance, and breathe out. Slowly bring the sole of one foot to rest on your standing leg, either above or below the knee. Try to balance while breathing in and out. If you want, you can extend your arms overhead while keeping your palms together. Next, try the pose using your other leg. This pose is great for your balance.

Flamingo

Flamingos live in warm, watery areas such as lagoons or lakes. They eat shrimps and tiny plantlike creatures called algae, which give them their bright pink color. Scientists think that flamingos might balance on one leg to keep warm—or they might just do it to be more comfortable!

Gorilla (also called standing forward fold): Uttanasana

If you want to stretch out your back, this is a great pose. Stand with your feet facing forward and slightly apart and take a big deep breath in. Breathe out and gently bend forward from your hips (not from your waist). Keep your knees slightly bent, and let your arms and head hang toward the floor. Rest here as you breathe in and out.

Mountain Gorilla

Mountain gorillas live on the volcanic mountains of Rwanda, Uganda, and the Democratic Republic of the Congo in Africa. They are social, and usually live in groups of about 30. Gorillas have long arms that hang to the ground and allow them to walk quickly on all fours.

Cat (also called cat pose): Marjaryasana

This is another pose that's good for your back! Start on your hands and knees with your hands under your shoulders and your knees under your hips. Spread your fingers wide. Breathe out and gently relax the top of your head toward the floor and round your spine upward. Breathe in and arch your spine, dropping your belly toward the floor and raising your head and tailbone up. (This is also known as bitilasana, or cow pose.) Do this as many times as you want, breathing in and out.

Domestic Cat

Domestic cats have lived as pets all around the world for thousands of years. Cats of all kinds arch their backs for several reasons: Sometimes they do this while hopping around to play; other times they do it when they are scared, to frighten off other animals. And sometimes they arch their backs just to stretch!

Puppy (also called downward dog): Adho Mukha Svanasana

Start on your hands and knees. Place your palms flat on the floor, shoulder-width apart, with your knees under your hips. Spread your fingers wide. Breathe out and press down through your feet and gently reach your "tail" up to the ceiling, forming an upside-down V. Relax your head and neck, and breathe in and out at your own pace. This pose can help you be more aware of your own body.

Domestic Dog

Though they are related to wild wolves, domestic dogs live all around the world as pets. They can be big or small; there are more than 300 breeds. Dogs often bow low to the ground and raise their hind ends to stretch—but they also do this when they want to play!

Lion (also called lion pose): Simhasana

Start by kneeling on the floor, and sit back with your hips on your heels. Bring your hands to the floor in front of you (or to your knees), and spread your fingers wide. Breathe in through your nose. Open your mouth and your eyes as wide as possible, stick out your tongue, and breathe out through your mouth. Lion pose is great for your confidence!

Lion

Lions are big cats that live in the deserts and grasslands across central and southern Africa. They live in groups called prides, and roar to communicate with each other. A lion's roar can be heard as far as five miles (8 km) away!

Bunny (also called rabbit pose): Sasangasana

This pose is great for stretching out your shoulders. Kneel on the ground and sit back on your heels. Lace your fingers behind your back. Take a big breath in, gently lean forward, and relax your body on top of your legs. Rest your head on the ground in front of you. Gently lift your arms behind you toward the sky. Breathe in and out.

Domestic Rabbit

Rabbits live in meadows, forests, grasslands, wetlands, and deserts, and domestic rabbits are kept as pets around the world. They are herbivores, and eat grasses and other plants. Rabbits often curl up to sleep, or—when they're especially happy—will jump into the air in a move called a binky.

Cobra (also called cobra pose): Bhujangasana

Cobra pose can make you stronger, and can also stretch your back. Lie on your tummy with your legs straight out behind you. Place your palms flat on the ground next to your shoulders. Keep your elbows tucked in toward your body, and press down slightly with the tops of your feet and your hips. Take a big breath in and gently lift your head, chest, and shoulders off the ground. Exhale and lie back down. Repeat as many times as you like.

Cape Cobra

Cape cobras live in the savannas and deserts of southern Africa. They are carnivores, and eat small animals like birds, frogs, and rodents. Cobras move by slithering across the ground. If threatened, a cobra will raise its head off the ground and spread its hood to appear larger and scare off any danger.

Crocodile (also called crocodile pose): Makarasana

If you want to relax, this is the pose for you! Lying on your belly, cross your arms in front of your head. Rest your forehead on your hands or arms, and let your whole body relax. Breathe deeply for six to ten breaths.

Nile Crocodile

Nile crocodiles are the second largest type of crocodile (after the salt-water), and can grow up to 20 feet (6 m) long and weigh up to 1,650 pounds (748 kg)! They live throughout parts of sub-Saharan Africa. Because crocodiles are cold-blooded, meaning they rely on their environment to keep warm, they often bask in the sun on their bellies.

To all my poetry teachers
—P.T.

Since 1888, the National Geographic Society has funded more than 12,000 research, exploration, and preservation projects around the world. The Society receives funds from National Geographic Partners, LLC, funded in part by your purchase. A portion of the proceeds from this book supports this vital work. To learn more, visit natgeo.com/info.

For more information, visit nationalgeographic.com, call 1-877-873-6846, or write to the following address:

National Geographic Partners
1145 17th Street N.W.
Washington, D.C. 20036-4688 U.S.A.

Visit us online at nationalgeographic.com/books

For librarians and teachers: nationalgeographic.com/books/librarians-and-educators

More for kids from National Geographic: natgeokids.com

National Geographic Kids magazine inspires children to explore their world with fun yet educational articles on animals, science, nature, and more. Using fresh storytelling and amazing photography, *Nat Geo Kids* shows kids ages 6 to 14 the fascinating truth about the world—and why they should care. **kids.nationalgeographic.com/subscribe**

For rights or permissions inquiries, please contact National Geographic Books Subsidiary Rights: bookrights@natgeo.com

ILLUSTRATIONS CREDITS
AL=Alamy; GI=Getty Images; MP=Minden Pictures; SS=Shutterstock

Front cover: (giraffe), jaroslava V/SS; (girl), Rebecca Hale/NG Staff; (rabbit), Vitaly Korovin/SS; (dog), fotojagodka/iStock/GI; (yoga mat), Gearstd/SS; (cat), Life On White/GI; **Back cover:** (giraffe), jaroslava V/SS; (dog), kozorog/GI; (lion cub), Eric Isselee/SS; **Interior:** (yogi kids throughout), Rebecca Hale/NG Staff; 2 (UP), kozorog/GI; 2 (LO), Gearstd/S; 5, Ben Rayner; 6 (UP), Ingo Arndt/MP; 6 (RT), John Warburton-Lee/GI; 6 (LO), Andre and Anita Gilden/GI; 8, Anup Shah/GI; 10, Natalia Barsukova/SS; 12, Thomas Marent/MP; 14 (UP), Alena Ozerova/SS; 14 (LO), Cultura Creative (RF)/AL; 15 (LO), Image by Chris Winsor/GI; 16, david pearson/AL; 18, Graham Swain/EyeEm/GI; 20 (LE), Phil McLean/MP; 20 (RT), age fotostock/AL; 21 (UP), Andrew Parkinson/GI; 22, Michael and Patricia Fogden/MP; 24, Mohamed Rageh/GI; 27 (UP LE), Paul Souders/GI; 27 (UP RT), Vicki Jauron, Babylon and Beyond Photography/GI; 27 (LO), Ben Queenborough/AL; 28 (LO LE), Anup Shah/GI; 28 (LO RT), Natalia Barsukova/S; 29 (LO LE), Thomas Marent/MP; 29 (LO RT), Cultura Creative (RF)/AL; 30 (LO LE), david pearson/AL; 30 (LO RT), Graham Swain/EyeEm/GI; 31 (LO LE), Phil McLean/MP; 31 (UP RT), Michael and Patricia Fogden/MP; 31 (LO RT), Mohamed Rageh/GI; design element (mandalas throughout book), Home/SS

Designed by Kathryn Robbins

The author would like to thank Kate Hale and Marfé Ferguson Delano, executive editors; Michaela Weglinski, assistant editor; Shannon Hibberd, senior photo editor; Alix Inchausti, production editor; Anne LeongSon and Gus Tello, design production assistants; Tara Stiles, founder of Strala Yoga and expert reviewer; and our kid models, in order of appearance: Yasmine (Cover, Flamingo, Cat); Nathan (Giraffe, Cobra); Dane (Gorilla, Lion); Jenna (Puppy, Crocodile); and Claire (Bunny).

Hardcover ISBN: 978-1-4263-3752-9
Reinforced library binding ISBN: 978-1-4263-3753-6

Printed in Malaysia
20/TWP/1